Go MAD About Employee Engagement

Jo Hutchinson

&

Rob Huntington

First published in Great Britain in 2013

Go MAD Books
Pocket Gate Farm
Off Breakback Road
Woodhouse Eaves
Leicestershire
LE12 8RS
United Kingdom

ISBN No 978-0-9551287-9-0

Contents

What Managers and Leaders are saying about this book

"Do you want to make a measurable difference to the engagement of your employees? This is one of the best possible resources to help you do this!"
Ian James, Training & Competence Manager

"It gives a clear and concise approach to taking on personal responsibility for engaging in your life and to make it better but also to take ownership of the 'engagement' in your workplace."
Jane Wisson, Customer Services Team Leader

"A great introduction to engagement with lots of helpful ideas."
Elaine Mulheron, Learning & Development Manager

"It will make you think about something you probably don't allow yourself time to think about i.e. Engagement."
Martyn Hooton, Technical Team Leader

"An essential guide for all of those managing and being managed that provides practical information that can be applied rather than general theory which gets ignored."
Nick Kay, Senior Finance Officer

"As with all the Go MAD books this is a practical guide packed with tips that can be put into practice straight away."
Derek Reynolds, Planning Manager

"Challenges your thinking on engagement and helps you to think through key aspects in a coherent way."
Howard Cain, Team Leader Proposition & Qualification Support

"An inspirational book to read."
Steve Poole, People Development Manager

"Accessible way to look at a complex issue, with tips, hints & guidance."
Anni Marland, Learning & Development Manager

"Read this – it will help you get a good appreciation of what 'engagement' is all about. It provides useful and practical tips for how to get started or build on what you're already doing."
Ainsley Allen, Director

"This discusses employee engagement at a personal level and uses this to illustrate other perspectives. The tips are very practical."
Guy Norris, Head of Business Management

"Clear and concise, easy to understand."
Donna Clark, Policy Officer

"It's a thought provoking, accessible book from which you can take and share learning."
Marion Nash, Head of Funding

"A different approach to exploring employee motivation and clarity of goals - it comes from a different angle."
Paul McKenzie, Head of Finance

FOREWORD
DO WE REALLY NEED ANOTHER BOOK ABOUT EMPLOYEE ENGAGEMENT?

Employee engagement is big business these days. A recent search on the Internet highlighted 5,370,000 results on Google and 2,005 books on Amazon. (By the time you read this, those numbers will have increased!) There are a multitude of surveys that measure indicators of employee engagement that organisations dedicate a huge amount of time and money to. It is the subject of many books, websites, government research papers and conferences to name but a few.

The link between employee engagement and the bottom line has now been well-researched and is understood. We'll share some of those statistics with you later.

So, if there is already a lot of information out there and the business case has been made, why write another book?

What will this book give you that others don't?

Two things

Firstly:
We work closely with organisations worldwide to help them achieve the results they want. In doing this we have noticed that many organisations conduct employee engagement surveys and have measurement actions in place. These activities on their own will not increase employee engagement.

It brings to mind a great phrase once used by an engineering director we worked with, "There is a danger of spending too much time weighing the pig instead of getting it ready for market". When he used this phrase he was talking about 'analysis paralysis'. So much time is spent considering the measures and figuring out different ways of looking at things when actually people would be better off doing something towards changing the results.

This book is here to help you practically and tangibly do something that will have a direct impact on increasing employee engagement. Consider it your toolkit.

Secondly:

The other thing we have noticed over the past 15 years is that the individuals and teams who consistently apply the unique Go M.A.D. ® Framework as a Results Focused Thinking System demonstrate the two key facets of employee engagement. Number one, that they are satisfied in their work and number two, that they positively and actively contribute to the organisation's vision and goals. So that got us thinking…

"What if we shared the Go M.A.D.® Results Focused Thinking System in a way that everyone could see the clear value and relevance as an employee engagement toolkit that REALLY works?"

This book is also going to show you how to apply the principles of our Thinking System in a practical way to employee engagement. If you are new to this you will find it a structured, common sense approach; however much of that common sense may not be common practice in your organisation. If you are already familiar with our Thinking System, then this book will help you view it with a different perspective. In addition it will give you new insights and ideas about how to use it to make a difference in your organisation.

Overall the purpose of this book is to show you the **'How to'** about employee engagement rather than the **'What is'** employee engagement.

How to get the most from this book

We encourage you to read it from two perspectives:

- As an **individual** employee, regardless of status and grade. Read it and ask, "What could I be doing to take personal responsibility for my OWN engagement?"

- As a **leader** (or if you do not have direct people responsibilities, as a colleague). Read it and ask, "What could I be doing to influence the engagement of OTHERS?" Whether that be your team or peers.

The book is structured so you can easily see the parts that apply to you as an individual and the parts that relate to you as a leader.

Also, you will see there are thinking activities to complete. Take the time to do these to deepen your understanding of your own and others' engagement. They will be useful activities to introduce to your own team. We also invite you to highlight, underline and scribble away in this book.

How we involved others

Before we get started, we'd like to point out that all the tips contained in this book are tried and tested. We have had the privilege of partnering with many like-minded people in many great organisations and we would like to thank everyone who has willingly contributed their knowledge and expertise towards this book.

Special thanks go to the group of Senior Leaders who joined us for an Organisational Development Thinking Day on the topic of employee engagement. Their discussions, thoughts and debates helpfully provoked our thinking on this topic, much of which is included in the following pages.

To answer our opening question

Do we really need another book about employee engagement?

Yes, because this one will work, but with one caveat. Reading alone will not make a difference – you have to take action. Make the choice now before you read more.

? *Ask Yourself*

What are you going to choose to do to make a difference to your own and others' engagement at work?

PART ONE

INTRODUCTION

THE CASE FOR EMPLOYEE ENGAGEMENT

"But I like to think that a lot of managers and executives trying to solve problems miss the forest for the trees by forgetting to look at their people – not at how much more they can get from their people or how they can more effectively manage their people. I think they need to look a little more closely at what it's like for their people to come to work there every day."

Gordon Bethune, Continental Airlines

The statistics speak for themself

There is much statistical data that makes the case that engaged employees make a difference to the bottom line. If you are in any doubt, here are some of the most powerful and hard hitting:

- The lost productivity of actively disengaged employees costs the US economy $370 billion annually. (Gallup)

  ? **Ask Yourself -** *How much might your lost productivity add up to annually?*

- A 1% increase in employee commitment can lead to a monthly increase of 9% in sales. (IES)

  ? **Ask Yourself -** *What impact would an increase of 9% in sales have on your organisation?*

- In 2009 an analysis of 199 surveys found that business units scoring in the top half of employee engagement doubled their odds of delivering high performance, compared to those in the bottom half. Those at the 99th percentile are nearly five times more likely to deliver high performance than those at the 1st percentile. (Gallup)

? **Ask Yourself -** *Would you describe your organisation as truly high performing?*

- A study of 115 companies suggested that a business with highly engaged employees achieves a financial performance four times greater than companies with poor engagement. In 2008/09 it was reported that highly engaged employees are more than twice as likely to be top performers – almost 60% of them exceed expectations for performance. (Watson Wyatt)

? **Ask Yourself -** *How many of your people exceeded on their performance objectives last year?*

- Engagement levels can be predictors of sickness absence, with more highly engaged employees taking an average of 2.7 days per year, compared with disengaged employees taking an average of 6.2 days per year. (Gallup)

? **Ask Yourself -** *What's the average number of days per year that your employees have for sickness absence?*

- Higher levels of engagement are strongly related to higher levels of innovation. 59% of engaged employees say that their job brings out their most creative ideas against 3% of disengaged employees. (Gallup)

? **Ask Yourself -** *How much new and innovative thinking do your people contribute?*

- Between 35% and 50% of employees in an organisation are disengaged at any one time. (Mclean & Company)

? **Ask Yourself -** *How many of your employees do you believe are disengaged right now?*

The Case for Employee Engagement

Marks and Spencer's research shows that over a four-year period stores with improving engagement had, on average, delivered £62 million more sales to the business every year than stores with declining engagement.

Sainsburys have also found clear links between higher levels of engagement and sales performance, with the level of colleague engagement contributing up to 15% of a store's year on year growth.

WHAT IS EMPLOYEE ENGAGEMENT?

Some definitions

What do we mean by the term 'employee engagement'? There are numerous definitions of employee engagement, the three we believe to be most relevant are:

"Employee engagement describes employees' emotional and intellectual commitment to their organisation and its success. Engaged employees experience a compelling purpose and meaning in their work and give their discrete effort to advance the organisation's objectives."

Work Foundation

"Employee engagement can be defined as an employees' drive to use all of their ingenuity and resources for the benefit of the organisation."

Best Companies

"Being focused in what you do (thinking), feeling good about yourself in your role and the organisation (feeling), and acting in a way that demonstrates commitment to the organisational values and objectives (acting)."

CIPD

A bit of history

The principles of engagement are not a new concept. There are indications that the concept has been around a long time as both the Greeks and Romans 'encouraged' their workers. However, employee engagement mainly comes from studies, which began in the 1920's, of morale or a group's willingness or reason to accomplish organisational objectives.

What makes the difference?

Employee engagement is about how people behave at work as a result of how they feel about the work. It refers to the extent to which people in an organisation know what they have to do, and willingly give their discretionary effort to do that. It is the difference between people coming to work and doing an adequate job, and people coming to work and really giving their best, displaying creativity and using their initiative.

Often the term 'employee engagement' is used interchangeably with phrases such as:

- Employee commitment
- Job satisfaction
- Employee happiness
- Internal communication.

The reality is that it is very much a combination of all of these things and one in isolation does not make for great employee engagement.

Categories of engagement

The Gallup Organisation interestingly defines three categories of engagement:

1. **The Engaged Employees**: people who work with a passion and feel a profound connection to their company. They drive innovation and move the organisation forward. They have a clear sense of ownership, satisfaction, purpose and pride in relation to their job. They are energised, enthusiastic, self-motivated and focus on the organisation's objectives, not just their own. They act as ambassadors for the organisation.

2. **The Non-Engaged Employees**: these are the people who Gallup describes as having 'checked out'. They are probably those who sleep walk their way through their days in your offices, retail outlets and factories. These people decided to 'quit and stay'. They put in the time but don't approach their work with energy and passion any more. They may lack the desire or ambition to genuinely care about their job or organisation; for them coming to work is like 'going through the motions'.

3. **The Actively Disengaged Employees**: these people are not just unhappy at work; they are busy acting out their unhappiness. Every day they undermine what engaged colleagues accomplish, and the real danger is they may be telling your customers about their disengagement too. Their focus will be on personal goals, as opposed to team or organisational best interests.

◌ *Time to Think about You*

Let's just pause for a moment. Take a look at those three descriptions. Which one best describes you at the moment? If you reviewed your last week at work, what evidence could you provide for each? It may be that engagement is situational and variable. How would your colleagues describe your engagement last week?

Use the space below to capture occasions in the last week when you demonstrated engagement, non-engagement and disengagement? What does this tell you about yourself that you might want to change?

CHARACTERISTICS OF ENGAGED AND DISENGAGED EMPLOYEES

To get a more practical real life definition of engagement we asked a group of leaders, across a range of different businesses, to describe the characteristics of engaged and disengaged employees. This is what they said:

Engaged I know I'm engaged when…	**Disengaged** I know I'm disengaged when…
• Getting up for work seems easier • I feel taken seriously and listened to • I put in the extra effort voluntarily because I 'care' • I feel valued • It made sense • I could see the reason for it • Someone told me I did a good job • Leaders come to me and share experiences • I can see I've made a difference • Relationships are stronger – I feel accepted and have professional friendships • I talk about the Company/job with pride to others • I feel a need to 'defend' my employer • I see high levels of engagement in others	• I'm unaware of what's going on • I don't feel valued • Change happens without communication • I feel indifferent • I have to 'armour up' to go to work • My work/life balance feels out of kilter and that I have 'no choice' • I am resentful to give the 'extra mile effort' • I talk about 'them' not 'us' • I feel let down • I feel a lack of support • I feel that both me and the organisation makes no progress • I don't understand the reason why for tasks • Communication channels are 'overgrown'

Engaged	**Disengaged**
I know I'm engaged when...	I know I'm disengaged when...
<ul><li>I have an emotional connection with the 'story' of the organisation's journey and vision</li><li>I do the extra work by choice</li><li>I didn't need a script when talking about the organisation's ambition</li><li>I care, connect and contribute</li><li>I see momentum and energy</li><li>Work matters, it's meaningful</li><li>I feel part of something bigger</li><li>I understand my role and how it fits</li><li>There is a congruence of values – personal and organisational</li><li>I have a future focus – I can see the end goal</li></ul>	<ul><li>I don't feel I have a 'professional friend'</li><li>I am feeling out of sync with the organisation in relation to my values</li><li>I personally feel I have outgrown the organisation</li></ul>

Time to Think about You

What about you? What are your characteristics when you are engaged or disengaged?

Think back to the previous activity when you captured situations when you felt engaged or disengaged. Think about high points and low points in your career.

What were you saying to yourself? What actions did you take or not take? Write your personal definition of engagement by completing the two columns below.

Engaged	Disengaged
I know I'm engaged when...	I know I'm disengaged when...

So far you have thought about a personal definition of engagement. But now let's consider completing those two statements from a leadership perspective.

Consider levels of achievement on business results, the types of questions and statements you hear people making, the recalled memories they refer back to and how they talk about the future. Also, think about how easy it is to make decisions, find information and what the atmosphere is like in the office or on the shop floor.

Engaged	Disengaged
I know people in my organisation are engaged when...	I know people in my organisation are disengaged when...

Now compare and contrast the two perspectives you have created – for yourself and as a leader. How many of the behaviours and actions are common across each list? This is about thinking as a leader about the 'engagement shadow' you cast. How many of the characteristics of your disengaged workforce are actually a reflection of your own disengagement, or the disengagement of others in the Leadership Team? If you are a leader then engagement starts with you at the top!

 Time to Think about You

Another great way to define engagement is to notice what people say when they talk about their day at work with their friends and family. Again we asked a group of leaders to imagine an engaged and disengaged employee completing the phrase, 'Today at work...' These are some of their suggestions:

Engaged	Disengaged
'Today at work...'	'Today at work...'
<ul><li>I had a great day</li><li>I did some great stuff</li><li>I made a difference</li><li>I added value and someone told me I did</li><li>I shared a really good idea</li><li>I contributed to the project</li><li>I acted like an owner</li><li>We had fun and laughed</li><li>I helped a customer</li><li>We won an award</li><li>I enjoyed it</li><li>I made things better</li><li>I learned something new</li></ul>	<ul><li>I was banging my head against a brick wall</li><li>No one was listening... again</li><li>I found a great holiday on the web</li><li>Time passed so slowly</li><li>...actually I don't want to talk about my day at work!</li><li>I don't care anymore</li><li>I couldn't be bothered</li><li>My work was boring</li><li>Enough is enough – I want to leave</li><li>I felt like I had nowhere to go</li></ul>

Engaged	Disengaged
'Today at work...'	'Today at work...'
• I helped someone out • I got momentum going on something • I found someone to help me	• My manager didn't understand me • My manager annoyed me • The team meeting made me feel deflated • I was confused about what was going on • I had a laugh and a joke with a customer about how bad it is there

Now think about what you said last night when you got home, write down your comments here.

Are they the comments of an engaged or disengaged employee?

? **Ask Yourself**
What do you want to take forward as a result of completing these activities?

EMPLOYEE ENGAGEMENT – WHAT IT ISN'T

It's worth pointing out here that there are a few things that employee engagement isn't.

- It's not an event, that is, something that happens when the survey is completed. The survey is a measure and snapshot of attitudes at the time. Engagement is something that both individuals and leaders need to think about on a daily basis. It needs to become a way of working. It's about the **HOW** as much as it's about the **WHAT**.

- It's not something that sits on your to-do list. Engagement is achieved through thinking and actions which in turn leads to results. It is not a task that you do on a Tuesday between 3.00 pm and 4.00 pm. It acts as an enabler for your to-do list as a way of getting things done faster, effectively and more innovatively.

- It's not a HR buzz word. It's a real catalyst for better business results. It may have risen to the top of business focus in the recent decade but it's been around for years.

- It's not just a set of actions that remove the 'dis-satisfiers' in an organisation: the broken down photocopier, the shortage of coffee cups, outdated technology, payroll errors, for example. These are things that cause annoyance and frustration for people and whilst it's important to address these 'dis-satisfiers', this only tackles peoples' 'away from' motivation by removing sources of pain. As a balance there also needs to be a set of actions that address peoples' 'towards' motivation – these are the satisfiers that lead to true engagement, the things that cause people to want to come to work, do a great job and stay with you.

- It's not something that only a few people are responsible for. Setting up an action team or a focus group can be a good idea to help clear obstacles, measure progress and implement some quick wins off the survey. However the risk with this approach is that it's easy for the other 99.5% of the population to sit back and wait for other people to improve engagement.

Who is responsible for it?

EVERYONE!

The Case for Employee Engagement

The Welsh Government launched the 'Managing with Less' initiative in January 2010, in response to a substantial reduction in the budgets available to run the organisation. Since it began, it has secured the active engagement of most of their 5,500 employees. 98% of employees were aware of the 'Managing with Less' initiative, 83% of employees participated in discussion sessions to generate cost-saving and efficiency-enhancing ideas, and 86% of employees felt that their colleagues were committed to the 'Managing with Less' approach.

A key part of the initiative involved briefing and training divisional leaders to talk their teams through the financial scenarios and the potential impacts of the reduction in budgets. This led to some very direct conversations about the benefits of cutting 'discretionary' areas of spend in order to save jobs. Team members were typically prepared to be much more radical in their approach to cost-saving than senior leaders.

During 2010-11 'Managing with Less' resulted in reductions in spend of more than £20 million.

EMPLOYEE ENGAGEMENT – THE WAY FORWARD

We believe that to increase employee engagement everyone can take responsibility for examining their own levels of engagement and take responsibility to make it better.

What if everyone in your organisation asked themselves the question, 'What am I going to do to make sure I am engaged today?' as they walked into the work place? That would make a difference wouldn't it?

But how many of your employees believe they are passive spectators (or even victims) in their own engagement? Perhaps they believe it's all down to someone else to make them feel better and more connected to the organisation. What if they never reflect on how their behaviour impacts on the engagement of their colleagues? We have actually met people who say they prefer it when certain colleagues are absent from work because of the effect they have on others' engagement levels!

So, it is important that people take **PERSONAL RESPONSIBILITY** to act at an **INDIVIDUAL** level.

The role of leaders

We also need to add in the impact of leaders. Again there is much data that states that people leave managers, not organisations. This suggests that the behaviour and actions of leaders will impact on employee engagement.

So, to complete the picture we need **LEADERSHIP RESPONSIBILITY** for employee engagement, to create the environment, conditions and culture that enables people to take **PERSONAL RESPONSIBILITY.**

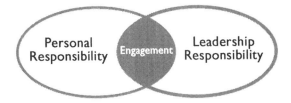

"The essence of competitiveness is liberated when we make people believe that what they think and do is important – and then get out of their way while they do it."

Jack Welch, General Electric

PART TWO

RESULTS FOCUSED THINKING

WHY YOU NEED A RESULTS FOCUSED THINKING APPROACH

"Employees will only complain or make suggestions three times on average without a response. After that they conclude that if they don't keep quiet they will be thought to be troublemakers or that management doesn't care."

Peter Drucker, Business Guru, Author, Professor of Business

The role of employee engagement surveys

For years, organisations have conducted employee engagement surveys to measure the perceptions of their employees, in order to understand their motivations and drivers. Surveys can be very useful in providing measurable results that can be tracked year-on-year. However, these are only aggregate results rather than individual engagement results, which is a distinction that should not be overlooked.

Sometimes the way survey data is used can decrease engagement. Very often there is a focus on unachievable and costly items such as large pay increases and the introduction of bonus schemes. Most organisations implement initiatives that treat symptoms and not root causes.

We have shown in the previous section that both individual and leadership responsibility impact on engagement. However, how many surveys and subsequent action groups focus on **both** of these areas?

A former colleague told the story of his well-intended but unpleasant experience of using his team's survey data to improve engagement. He called a meeting to share his business results with his managers and their direct reports. The group broke into teams to talk about the data. Inevitably the conversations turned towards the low 'scoring' areas, those responsible for them, and why the areas were mostly out of their control. He then asked the group to create a list of things to do to address the problems.

They created actions that no one was very excited about or really believed would make a difference. He realised the meeting and subsequent conversations got people to focus on what was wrong with the organisation. Engagement didn't improve and some would say it got worse. It is clear that the actions to address the 'problems' were reactive to the results. There was little or no focus on enabling people to take personal responsibility for their levels of engagement or for leaders to address the root cause.

Have you ever noticed this pattern of behaviour in organisations?

The employee engagement survey results are published. There are some high scoring areas and some areas that need attention. Frustratingly the areas that need attention are the same ones that needed attention last year, and the year before that. There is a small percentage shift but nothing transformational. This is known already because the atmosphere, the attitudes and the way the work gets done hasn't tangibly changed.

Business results aren't markedly different. The organisation sets up some groups dedicated to achieving new heights in employee engagement. They spend some months investigating the data (which is what the groups did last year). Some months have passed and it becomes difficult for the groups to meet because people have a perceived day job that doesn't include employee engagement. The remaining group members come up with a set of actions (not dissimilar to previous years) with mixed visible top leadership role modelling and support.

The survey is completed again

The employee engagement results are published. There are some high scoring areas and some areas that need attention. Frustratingly the areas that need attention are the same ones that needed attention last year, and the year before that. There is a small percentage shift but nothing transformational. This is known already because the atmosphere, the attitudes and the way the work gets done hasn't tangibly changed. Business results aren't markedly different. The osets up some groups dedicated to achieving new heights in employee engagement. They spend some months investigating the data (which is what the groups did last year).

Some months have passed and it becomes difficult for the groups to meet because people have a perceived day job that doesn't include employee engagement. The remaining group members come up with a set of actions (not dissimilar to previous years) with mixed visible top leadership role modelling and support.

Now you could be forgiven for thinking we just printed the same paragraph twice! Which we did - to make the point that this is what happens in some organisations:

Going around in a circle

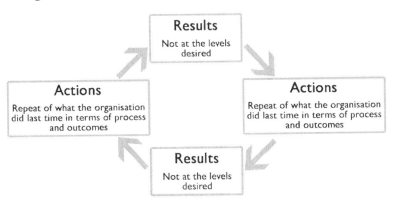

They don't get the results they want but they put in place the same set of actions, even though they didn't work last time. The results from those actions are not what was desired, so the same set of actions are put in place, which yet again yield the same results, and so on and so on. It's like an employee engagement Groundhog Day!

Focus on the thinking

What is needed is **DIFFERENT RESULTS**. To get different results you will need **DIFFERENT ACTIONS**. To get different actions you need **DIFFERENT THINKING**, as current thinking is not getting the results required.

We know from the extensive research we have carried out, that the nature of people's thinking; the speed, consistency, creativity and quality will have a direct impact on the actions they take and subsequently the results. That's why we created the unique Go M.A.D.® Framework as a Results Focused Thinking System. This Thinking System can be applied to any goal you want to achieve or difference you want to make.

Now we will move on to showing how applying the Go M.A.D.® Results Focused Thinking System can increase employee engagement for you, both as an individual and as a leader.

AN EMPLOYEE ENGAGEMENT THINKING SYSTEM

The Go M.A.D.® Research

In 1998 we undertook more than 4000 hours of research, interviewing people to find the answer to the following question:

"What is the simplest way of explaining the success process that people naturally use when making a difference?"

From this came seven principles for success linked together as a framework with 11 link lines.

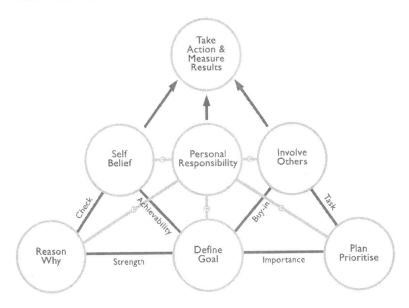

The Go M.A.D.® Framework

This is a systems thinking approach which means you need all the component parts of the system in place to increase your likelihood of success.

RESULTS FOCUSED THINKING FOR INDIVIDUAL ENGAGEMENT

Let's build this up principle by principle in relation to **AN INDIVIDUAL'S ENGAGEMENT** to demonstrate the systems thinking approach, starting with Reason Why.

Start with the Reason Why

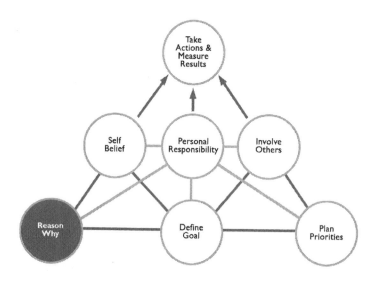

Reason Why is all about an individual's level of passion, excitement and motivation to achieve something. Naturally we all have different levels of motivation for the different things we have to do. Those levels can fluctuate throughout the day, week and year. We all know what it feels like to work on something we're excited about and we all know what it feels like to work on something we are not bothered about!

So, for engagement this is your first principle – feeling motivated. But is that enough?

Have something to achieve

That motivation needs to be aligned with and directed towards a goal or something that needs to be achieved. In organisations this is a work related goal. This provides purpose and focus and aligns personal motivation with the motivation of the organisation. Imagine a motivated employee who doesn't direct that passion towards achieving the organisational goals. You wouldn't describe them as engaged. Neither would an employee who describes themselves as motivated but has no clearly defined goal to work on. Not being able to see how they add value would be frustrating for them.

We now have two principles – motivation and a clearly defined goal. Is that enough to achieve engagement? What if the individual feels motivated, knows what it is they have to achieve BUT they have low belief in either themselves or others that the goal can be achieved?

Build Belief

Self-Belief, the confidence that a goal can be achieved is also required. Now we start to see the combination of hearts (Reason Why) and minds (Self-Belief) focused on the achievement of the goal (Define Goal).

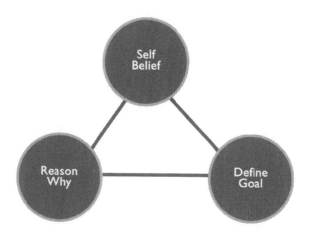

So, now we have an individual who is motivated, confident and has focus. Does that equate to engagement? What if they feel motivated, confident and know the goal but they are not prepared to take personal responsibility for making it happen?

Take Personal Responsibility

We have all probably come across those individuals (and we might have been one ourselves) who blame the organisation and circumstances, saying, "It's not down to me to make that happen – it's not my job." They don't sound like the words of an engaged employee, so let's add in the next principle of Personal Responsibility.

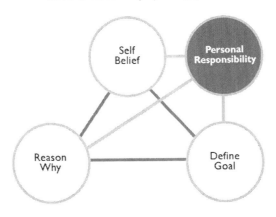

Personal Responsibility is about the individual asking the question, "Will I do this?" and answering unequivocally "yes!" It's about having the awareness that there are always choices, especially around thinking, and not blaming or adopting a victim mind-set when something doesn't happen.

Time to Think as a Leader

Just pause for a minute and think about employee engagement in your organisation. What percentage of your employees take Personal Responsibility for feeling and acting engaged whilst at work? On the other hand what percentage blame their manager, their working environment, the customer, the suppliers or their pay, and expect others to 'make them feel engaged'?

What if an extra 10%, 20% or 50% of people took Personal Responsibility for their own levels of engagement through using a Results Focused Thinking System? Surely that would make a difference to the business results in your organisation!

Key areas to diagnose disengagement

When we look at these four principles together they become an internal set of principles for people and a set of four bases from which a leader can diagnose causes of disengagement. This enables leaders to start to use the systems thinking approach with them.

Remove one and ask whether that would result in a fully engaged person? You'll find that you need all four in place.

Look externally

Now let's add in the other principles on the right-hand side of the Go M.A.D.® Framework and combine these with the four we have already looked at. As we move across to the right-hand side the principles are now external to the individual. This means they are about how they can engage with other people and the practicalities of how to make the goal happen.

Think Possibilities, Prioritise and Plan

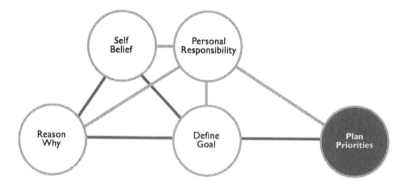

The principle Plan Priorities is about the 3P's:

1. **Possibility** thinking – engaging the imagination to generate a huge number of ideas, being creative and letting the brain get to the different thinking. This, in turn, will lead to different actions and different results.

   ? **Ask Yourself -** *How much new thinking is generated in your problem solving discussions?*

2. **Prioritising** those possibilities – deciding which of the ideas that have been generated are important to the achievement of the goal.

   ? **Ask Yourself -** *How many people do you see in your organisation prioritising activities that are NOT important for the achievement of the goal?*

3. **Planning** in time for the priorities – building and scheduling time during the working day to make sure the priorities are achieved. After all, they are the ones important to the goal.

   ? **Ask Yourself -** *How much time do people, in your organisation, spend working on activities that are not priorities and do not move the organisation towards its goal?*

Using each of the 3P's in relation to the goal can help to boost Self-Belief and motivation as people start to be able to see a tangible route to success. They are given the freedom to think through possibility thinking and they know that their time is well spent on meaningful tasks for the organisation.

Later when we look at the Go M.A.D.® Leadership Thinking Framework you'll see the importance of leaders at the top of organisations removing red tape, bureaucracy and other obstacles to free up people's time to work on the priorities.

So, with those five principles in place, is that enough for employee engagement?

Determine who can help

The success of any goal will depend on to what extent the Involve Others principle is applied. The importance of getting the buy-in of others through a strong Reason Why will be a success factor. The people involved in our original research thought about the reasons to possibly Involve Others, who they might be, how to communicate the goal to them and get their buy-in.

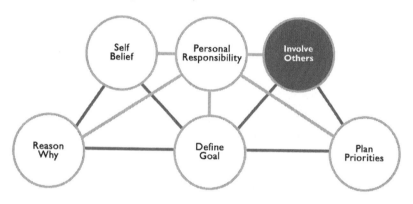

Knowing there is a need to do some thinking about Involving Others, to ensure the goal is achieved, is crucial. It's all part of the HOW. Actively thinking about this principle will mean the employee is less likely to hit people-related hurdles and barriers that may cause engagement levels to drop. It's also about being a great colleague and having great working relationships – those relationships that lead to the work getting done in the most efficient and effective way yet still gives satisfaction to the employees.

Look internally and externally

Personal Responsibility and Define Goal are shared in both the internal and external employee engagement view of the Go M.A.D.® Framework.

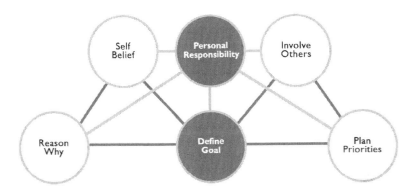

This is because the engaged employee is aware of and considers two things:

1.   The Personal Responsibility they need to take internally to build their own motivation and Self-Belief levels, with the need to keep a check on those levels from time-to-time. In addition they take Personal Responsibility for choosing to make a difference, take on the goal and seek clarity if the goal appears ambiguous at first.

2.   The Personal Responsibility they need to take to create ideas, and plan in time to complete the priorities. Plus, defining and sharing the goal with others in a way that gets their buy-in and causes their engagement to increase.

Do something

The six principles we have introduced so far, if adopted by the individual, still have something missing. They cover internal and external perspectives, what's left is to Take Action and Measure Results. This is about doing something, however small, towards the goal being achieved. It's about momentum and celebrating the wins along the way by measuring progress.

All good practice which ultimately builds engagement.

Without taking action, it's just been thinking!

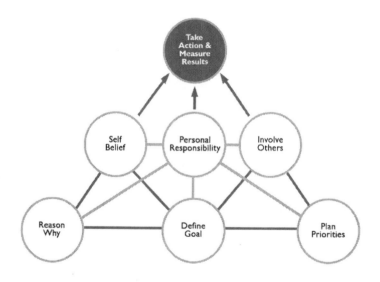

Now we have the complete Go M.A.D.® Framework built with its seven principles and eleven link lines, which when consistently applied, will increase your probability of engagement success. You now have your employee engagement Thinking System. You're possibly thinking that it's all common sense – and it is! But as we said earlier, how often is common sense, common practice in your organisation?

Why things can go wrong

One of the most common organisational behaviour patterns we observe is the application of the three central column principles only.

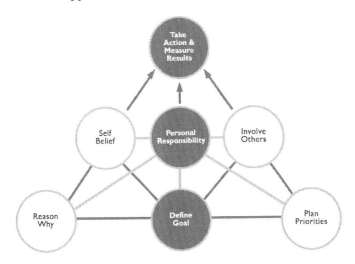

People are given the goals, told to take Personal Responsibility for making them happen, left to take action and then have their results measured at their performance reviews. Whilst it is possible to achieve results by only applying these three principles, it will take longer and feel more difficult. Additionally, the results may not be as sustainable with levels of innovation and different thinking being low.

This is because engagement levels will be lower as a result of not paying attention to all seven principles. Make sure you are taking opportunities to build employee engagement and constantly check that you and others have all seven principles in place.

Engagement is not an action or an event. It's not something that is achieved through scheduling in an employee engagement review every month. It's helping you and others to adopt a Results Focused Thinking approach. It's something that everyone can easily take responsibility for.

Some good news

To end this section – some good news! The likelihood is that when you are successful you are already applying all these principles so you already know how to use them.

More good news

Secondly, now you know about the principles forming a thinking system you can choose to consciously apply them. By applying them to your engagement levels and that of others, you will increase your likelihood of success.

The Case for Employee Engagement

RSA is a multinational insurance group employing 23,000 people. Research in their 'MORE TH>N' call centres has shown that engaged people have 35% lower average wrap times (time between calls) than disengaged people.

Engaged staff are able to talk to, on average, an additional 800 customers per year (based on an average call handling time of 365 seconds). Put another way, for every eight engaged people they employ they get the equivalent of an additional member of staff without any increase in the wage bill.

PART THREE

TOP TIPS

TOP TIPS TO INCREASE EMPLOYEE ENGAGEMENT

In this section we'll give you practical suggestions of how to increase employee engagement. These tips relate to each principle of the Go M.A.D.® Framework and are either for you to apply for yourself or to help you as a leader. They are all tried and tested and if applied you will make a difference!

 ## Reason Why

Having a strong Reason Why is the engine room of momentum and pace. A participant on one of our programmes once said, "All people are lazy." But is it laziness or just a lack of Reason Why?

We meet people who achieve amazing things for themselves and others outside of work, yet as they cross the threshold into work they appear to leave their drive and desire in the car park. These tips will help you to consider what you can do to help lift the motivation of others or yourself. Think about it, working with a demotivated colleague or boss is probably not the favourite part of people's jobs.

"Without inspiration the best powers of the mind remain dormant. There is a fuel in us which needs to be ignited with sparks."
Johann Gottfried Von Herder

✱ Tips for You

1. Keep a check on your personal levels of Reason Why. Use a 1 to 10 scale where 1 is low and 10 is high. If your motivation is low how might that impact on the motivation levels of others around you? Ask the question, "What could I possibly do today to increase my motivation?" Then take action on at least one idea.

2. Work on what excites you. Excitement precedes passion. If possible reduce the work that doesn't excite you. Think about something you feel passionate about outside of work. Identify what causes you to feel passionate about this and consider how you could replicate that at work.

3. Decide how bothered you want to be. Reason Why is quite simply about how bothered you are. If you hear your internal self-talk saying, "I can't be bothered", answer that back with, "What difference could I make if I was bothered?"

4. Understand that the Reason Why is likely to be higher if the work you do and the organisation you work for are a good match for your values. How could you ensure that your time at work enables you to live your values on a day-to-day basis?

5. Ask yourself, "What is the motivational kick up the backside that I might possibly need to give myself?"

6. Consider how you will know when your Reason Why levels are dropping. Learn to spot the early warning signs of this so you can address it quickly before it's too late.

7. Monitor it in the same way as you would hard business metrics. For example, you'd be able to spot early on if your sales started to drop. So, also look out for dips in motivation.

8. Decide whether to be a whining dog or not. In his bestselling book, 'Go MAD – the art of making a difference' Andy Gilbert tells the story of the 'whining dog'. This dog sits on a nail which hurts, but it doesn't move to sit somewhere else, it just whines. This story equates to the person who is not sick and tired enough yet, of being sick and tired, to do something about the source of the pain. What is the pain that causes you to whine? When will you reach the level that you are bothered enough to do something about it? Make a choice today – to whine or not to whine!

9. Recognise your blind spots. What are the things that you say and do, or don't say and do, that impact on yours and others' motivation? When you make these self-discoveries commit to doing something different.

10. Find ways to hold up the mirror to yourself so you can see your motivational blind spots.

11. Have a look around you at work today. Who is the person in your organisation who is the biggest motivating force for you? Have you spoken to them recently? Maybe today is the day you go for a coffee with them to get an injection of motivation. Remember to ask what you can do to help them as well!

12. Be consistently authentic when you go to work, that is, be yourself! This will lead you to be more effective by being more relaxed and open.

13. Avoid that 'Sunday night feeling', that sensation of dread as Monday morning and work approaches. Make the choice to change that feeling. What if the Sunday night feeling was one of excitement about the week ahead? Imagine your week going well. Use the tips in the Define Goal section to set yourself up for success.

14. Discover how to fall back in love with your job. Yes, you read that right. After a period of time, people can lose the initial excitement and enthusiasm they had for a job and organisation that they had when they started. In effect they fall out of love with their job and, just like in a relationship, take less care and attention over things, develop some bad habits, get comfortable and take things for granted. If that sounds like you, find ways to fall back in love with your job.

15. Tidy up those piles of paper on your desk that have been sitting there for over a year. Smarten up your thinking and approach to tasks. Recall all those great habits you had when you started and implement them again.

⭐ *Tips for Leaders*

16. Find out what people's 'Reason Why' to come to work is. If they haven't got one, help them find one.

17. Get your team members to identify something that they are passionate about outside of work. Ask them to think about how they could possibly replicate this in the workplace.

18. Use what individuals are passionate about as a metaphor to fire up their imagination. For example, if someone is passionate about football you could describe the team and the goals to be achieved as a metaphor in relation to this.

19. Check if you and your team have a 'towards' motivation. Is there an appetite and hunger to move towards organisational and personal goals? Consider ways in which you can make the end point of the goal look like a great place to be. Paint the picture using words, images, metaphors or quotes to make it as vividly appealing to the senses as possible.

20. Consider different ways to capture emotions in your communication. This could be through story-telling, creating a picture, using a metaphor or recreating game shows with a twist, to name a few. This is more likely to capture hearts as well as minds than sitting through a long PowerPoint presentation.

21. Engage people in the dramatic stories of the business, the myths and legends that people still talk about. Bring the strategic ideas and issues to life in a language that makes sense for ALL employees.

22. Seek to understand the values of the people around you at work. What might you be doing that could compromise their values? What could you do to help them bring their values to life at work?

23. Find out what people are gossiping about in your organisation. Build your understanding of what these conversations reveal about how they really feel about being at work.

24. Capitalise on opportunities to motivate yourself and others in both formal and informal settings.

25. Identify the early warning signs of dips in motivation for each individual in your team. Work with them to understand what these might be. Also identify remedies to deal with the issues before they become serious. If their motivation dips, it is easier for a person to move from a 7 to an 8 on their 1 to 10 scale (of strength of Reason Why) than if it dips to a 2.

26. Consider how you can help to make people's life at work more rewarding. Find out what this would mean for them. Reward at work can be a tricky thing to get right. It can mean different things to different people. Understanding and exploring this is a good starting point.

27. Take the time to get to know the stories of the people you lead. Discover key things including: Where did they grow up? What are their interests outside of work? Favourite films and music? Also, let people have the opportunity to hear your story so that you are engaging with each individual.

28. Help your team avoid that 'Sunday night feeling'. If the majority of the organisation comes into work on a Monday morning with feelings of dread, you reduce your likelihood of achieving the results you want in your business that week.

29. Take leadership responsibility for enabling your team to have more helpful thoughts. Determine what would be the most helpful impact you could make at the very start of the working week.

30. Look for ways to strengthen people's motivation by providing development opportunities on a weekly basis. A person will feel more engaged if they truly believe, through the organisation's actions, that they have opportunities to grow, develop and achieve their potential.

31. Ensure that all employees understand the organisational Reason Why. Help them to understand: why the organisation exists, the strategic aims, the role it plays in society and the world. This last point is becoming increasingly important as talent is drawn to the organisations that have clear corporate and social responsibility policies. Ensure you are able to give this information.

✔ Time to Take Action

Which three tips will you take action on?
Use the table below to define your goals.

Tip no.	What specifically will you achieve?
By when?	Success measures
Tip no.	What specifically will you achieve?
By when?	Success measures
Tip no.	What specifically will you achieve?
By when?	Success measures
What else from this tips section do you want to remember?	

Define Goal

You get what you focus on. Clearly defined goals are essential to effective people related questionnaires and people based standards such as Investors in People. Yet the whole process of defining and communicating clear goals is sometimes overlooked.

Consider this as if you were a world-class athlete. Would the most successful athletes have achieved as much if they hadn't had something to aim at? We find that many people aim at nothing and hit it with incredible accuracy! These tips will help you to think about how having focus impacts on increasing employee engagement.

"Success is the sum of small efforts, repeated day in and day out."

Robert Collier

 **Tips for You**

32. Be **SPECIFIC** in your goal defining. Be absolutely clear about **WHAT** it is you want, rather than what you don't want.

33. Think in detail about what the **MEASURABLE** difference will be. Determine the tangible evidence that will show the added value to the organisation. Clearly identify the real end result.

34. Ensure that when identifying the measurable difference that the goal is achievable. Some organisations have adopted the concept of 'stretch' goals. These can work providing you have more belief than doubt that the goals are possible to **ACHIEVE**. You

will be more successful with goals that have a high level of achievability.

35. Keep all goals **RELEVANT**. Make sure they link to the bigger picture of the organisation.

36. Build in the **TIME** element to your goals so they state by when they will be achieved. Explore how you can use a range of timescales from 30 minute goals to longer-term goals that are five to 10 years out. Somebody who only has goals that take 10 years to achieve is a long time waiting to celebrate success!

37. The last few tips are about the **SMART** goal defining method. Check how **SMART** your goals are for today, this week and next year. If there was a test for SMARTness of objectives would your goals pass?

38. Write your goals down. A goal written down is more likely to be achieved than one that isn't.

39. Use language that is inspiring and motivational when forming your goals. Include action orientated verbs such as implement, design, identify and complete, to suggest movement and clear end results.

40. Think of achieving goals as 'wins'. Each step towards the goal is a win. Celebrate these wins along the way to achieving the overall goal.

41. Adopt a winning mind-set. Think about how many wins you had yesterday. Consider how satisfied you are with your number of wins.

42. Create some goal defining habits. Start by defining how many wins you want today.

43. Learn to think differently about what a win might be. It could be:

   - Finally achieving the financial sign-off you've been waiting months for
   - Finding time to have some lunch
   - Having the team meeting finish on time
   - Completing the actions from last week's meeting
   - Getting three new ideas from a colleague.

   How many wins are you going for today?

44. Notice how you feel when you achieve your wins. Also notice that now you are focused on having wins how they seem to appear everywhere!

45. Create goals each day that tackle different things. For example, you could have the 'I finally did it goal', for the thing that you have been putting off. You could have the 'wow goal' for things, if achieved, that would make you go 'wow'. You could have a 'new ideas goal' for the number of new ideas you generate in a day. These are just three suggestions, the possibilities are endless. Decide which type of goals you want to define for yourself today.

46. Make goal defining a habit for success. Out of work, define yourself goals when exercising, for example; how far do you want to run, how many calories do you want to burn, how many lengths do you want to swim in 30 minutes. Define yourself goals for your household and family activities. Define goals for anything you want to achieve so it becomes second nature.

47. Build yourself a wish list. What are all the things you might possibly want to achieve over the course of the next few years? The list could include dreams and aspirations as well as challenges to be overcome.

48. Pose the question, 'How could I possibly celebrate my successes?' and answer it 20 times. Pick some ideas off that list and put them into action.

Tips for Leaders

49. Ensure all goals defined are unambiguously clear. Check the SMARTness of all goals agreed with others.

50. Explain how achieving the goals will add value. Help others understand how their role has real purpose so that they feel more engaged.

51. Simplify the goal processes. Leaders often pass on too many goals. Work related goals, supplemented by stretch goals, transformation goals, personal development goals or change goals can just be too much. This results in not knowing where to start and how to prioritise what's important, with confusion possibly leading to disengagement.

52. Aim to create the simplest performance management processes possible. This will enable others to articulate their vital few priorities that are important to ensure the organisation achieves its goals.

53. Agree goals that enable the team to have successes and wins. Celebrating makes people feel good! Celebrations don't need to be big fanfare blowing events. They can be as simple as a collective 'pat on the back', buying a chocolate bar, going for lunch together as a team or giving the team five minutes in a

meeting to bask in their achievements. What could be other possible ways for you and the people you lead to celebrate wins?

54. Shift results by focusing a whole team around one activity for the day, week or month. For example, you could get everyone focused on doing something to shift productivity results, selling something in particular, bringing a brand value to life. What do you want people focusing on today? Help them to define a **SMART** goal so they have clarity of what is expected.

55. Check the reaction when others hear the words 'stretch goals'. Notice your own reaction to those words. Assess if this term causes helpful or hindering thoughts. If others are having hindering thoughts and you still want to continue with the essence of what stretch goals do, identify a more helpful way of describing them.

56. Make sure people know how what they do links to the bigger picture of the team and organisation. Consider how you can show pictorially how everyone's goals link together to add up to collective success. This again will help people to understand where they add value to the organisation. The Go MAD Thinking goal defining technique of 'umbrella goals' is really effective for this. (Learn more about this technique in the book, 'Go MAD About Coaching'.)

57. Emphasise the role and contribution each individual can make when briefing a new vision or long-term goal. Let them know their respective talents and unique value.

58. Describe your vision of where you want the team to be a month, year, and five years from now. This vision should be compelling and inspiring to ensure the team can't wait to be a part of delivering it. Be clear about the role and contribution

each individual can make by reviewing their talents and the value they can add.

59. Seek commitment rather than compliance. Help your team align the purpose of their work with the purpose and direction of the business.

60. Encourage your team to write a wish list. Help them to identify the hopes and aspirations that they have for the team or Department in the future. Ownership of the wish list strengthens Reason Why which in turn strengthens engagement.

✔ Time to Take Action

Which three tips will you take action on?
Use the table below to define your goals.

Tip no.	What specifically will you achieve?
By when?	Success measures
Tip no.	What specifically will you achieve?
By when?	Success measures
Tip no.	What specifically will you achieve?
By when?	Success measures
What else from this tips section do you want to remember?	

Self-Belief

How we talk to ourselves and others, the things we remember and imagine, can make a huge difference to how we feel about being at work and our responsibilities. How often do you find yourself talking yourself out of something, either putting it off or telling yourself that you'll never be able to achieve it?

We know that our thinking drives the actions we take, which in turn determines the outcome. So, if you think a target is impossible, then your actions will support that belief. And the resulting outcome? Yes, you've guessed it, the target is not achieved.

These tips help you to build employee engagement for yourself and others by showing you how to create belief and confidence that will give inspiration throughout the day. This means that not only will others leave with the feeling of having had a good day, but they will have been more productive too.

"The happiness of your life depends upon the quality of your thoughts; therefore guard accordingly."

Marcus Aurelius

⭐ Tips for You

61. Learn to spot the difference between helpful and hindering thoughts. Helpful thoughts are results focused and keep you moving towards the goal. Hindering thoughts tend to be more problem focused and do not move you towards the goal.

62. Catch yourself when you have hindering thoughts and ask yourself, "What would be a more helpful, results focused thing to say at this moment?"

63. Write down all your thoughts, now, helpful or hindering, about what you have to achieve this week. Sometimes just getting these thoughts down on paper can be quite cathartic. Take each hindering thought and flip it into a helpful thought by asking a results focused helpful question, for example:

> *Hindering thought*: "I'll never be able to get the budget signed off for this."
> *Helpful question*: "What could I possibly do to get the budget signed off?" or "Who could possibly help me get the budget signed off?"

64. Make some decisions about your hindering thoughts using the Control, Influence and Given model. Take each hindering thought and ask:

> Is this something I have **CONTROL** over? If the answer is yes, then decide whether this is something you want to take personal responsibility for and take some action. If the answer is no, then ask the next question.

> Is this something I could **INFLUENCE**? Again, if the answer is yes, take personal responsibility for finding ways you could influence the situation. If the answer is no then ask the next question.

> Have I made some **ASSUMPTIONS** about what I can really control and influence? Challenge yourself to question long-standing beliefs you may have about yourself and others. If after challenging your assumptions your answer to the first two questions is still no, then ask the next question.

> Is this a **GIVEN**? Something which I can neither control nor influence? If so, choose to accept the situation and

free up your thoughts to concentrate on more productive things.

Use this approach in team settings and one-to-ones.

65. Make a timeline of your successful memories. Use pictures and images to visually represent what happened. Remember to leave space on the timeline to add the successes of the future.

66. Adopt the Go M.A.D.® Results Focused Thinking System as a way of practically addressing worries. You cannot change the past, and worrying about the future will spoil the present. Look at your worries and consider if they are real or imagined. It has been estimated that up to 96% of worries and fears are unnecessary, either because they will never happen; they are groundless; or are from the past. And of the worries that are real around half of these will be out of your control.

67. Ignore hindering messages from others. It may be that your leader or others tell you repeatedly how difficult things are. Recognise that you have a choice whether to have helpful or hindering thoughts and you are in control of what you say to yourself.

68. Abolish the word 'try'! Are you the kind of person who 'tries' to get something done? Do you hear people in meetings say they will 'try' to get the action completed? Does your organisation 'try' to be best in class but never quite seems to make it? The word 'try' can indicate a lack of engagement, linked to self-belief, in the goal.

69. Establish the root cause of the word 'try' and take action to address it. This will increase confidence and lead to a more positive outcome, which can then be celebrated.

70. Take responsibility for your own happiness. Your job is an activity that you spend a lot of time on. Ask yourself some questions:

- Why do I work here?
- Why did I take the job in the first place?
- What is the purpose of my job?
- How does it impact the business?

Every job impacts some part of a business and therefore is an important job. It is great if everyone in the company sees that, but it is important for you to understand it.

- What do you enjoy about it?
- What would make it more fun?

The answers to these questions can help you focus on you and your happiness.

71. Refuse to give those you work with the power to wreck your day. Some people enjoy being miserable, but it doesn't have to be you. And if it's your boss who is the issue then mentally fire them.

✶ Tips for Leaders

72. Give people the awareness of the choices they have. Let them know that it is up to them whether they have helpful or hindering thinking. Hindering thoughts are contagious, especially in group settings, such as meetings, or around the coffee machine. This can have a knock on effect in causing disengagement.

73. Helpful thoughts are just as contagious. Build them into your 'rules of engagement' for team events, meetings and workplace environments. Helpful thoughts are pragmatic and future focused so are great for giving people a sense of progress.

74. Ask the question, "Is that helpful or hindering?" This will help others to build awareness of their thinking.

75. Avoid dwelling on previous failures and dredging them up and raking them over at every opportunity. This is never good for employee engagement. Get those hindering memories reframed into helpful ones by asking what lessons can be learned for the future and what could be changed as a result.

76. Listen to the language you use on a daily basis. We often hear leaders tell teams repeatedly how hard and difficult a task is going to be. This creates a hindering imagined future for people of having to work long hours, wading through problems and battling with others to get the work done.

77. Think about different ways you can present the message that will give people helpful self-talk about the future. For example, tough targets can still be exciting, rewarding, fun, great opportunities to learn and work together, to increase your competitiveness and be ground breaking. Which words would you choose?

78. Imagine if you or your team dealt with an internal or external customer with a head full of hindering thoughts either about themselves, the situation or indeed the customer! What will that customer experience feel like? Build the approach of helpful and hindering thoughts into your customer service programmes and initiatives.

79. Create an environment for the team, where they can share their hindering thoughts and turn them into helpful thoughts. Introduce hindering thoughts 'check-ins' at the start of meetings, invite people to share all their thinking at the outset, helpful and hindering.

80. Do some detective work and ask people what they are thinking. When they reply, ask yourself, "Am I hearing helpful or hindering thoughts?" And if they are hindering, "What could I do to help them?"

81. Make it part of your culture to talk through hindering thoughts openly as a way of overcoming problems. Sometimes people feel that they will be perceived as negative if they share hindering thoughts. As a result they hold on to them, possibly sharing them with colleagues (and potentially customers). Left unchecked they can become even bigger.

82. Train yourself to listen out for assumptions and self-limiting beliefs in yourself and others. When you think you hear one, ask the question, "What evidence is there to support that?" Beliefs are not always facts.

83. Help people understand how their own thinking can get in the way of them being the best they can be.

84. Collect the helpful memories of your organisation. Great memories are brilliant for building self-belief and creating a culture of success that people will want to be associated with. Was it when you won that industry award? Or when you achieved record levels of production? Or you won a big contract? Or when the team worked hard to deliver a project on time?

85. Remind people of these helpful memories to encourage helpful thinking. As well as making a timeline of your successful memories for yourself, get your team to make one.

86. See your written communication through others' eyes. Assess if it generates helpful or hindering thinking for the reader. Consider:

- How much does it make others want to engage?
- What questions might it possibly raise?
- What memories could it possibly trigger for them?
- What will their thinking about the future be as a result of reading it?
- Will these thoughts be helpful or hindering?

If the answer is hindering then tailor and bespoke your communication to address those hindering thoughts. For example, by referencing a helpful recalled memory.

87. Help build self-belief levels at times of change. It can be challenging to keep levels of engagement high due to hindering thinking about the future and perceived helpful thoughts about the past. You may feel that people refer back to the past as 'the good old days'. This is natural, as part of transition, as people come to terms with what has ended and experience a sense of loss with what they may have felt comfortable with in the past. Give people the opportunity to discuss and share these endings (without necessarily over promoting how great the future is going to be) so they can have them acknowledged in order to move on.

88. Identify ways in which you can physically mark an ending for people to help with closure. For example, if you are moving locations there may be artefacts that can be taken as mementoes, maybe even some of the bricks themselves if the building is coming down! It could be a team photo in the old location that you put up in the new location.

89. Ask the team to do some possibility thinking about how they would like to commemorate their endings and then prioritise into action.

90. Capture people's imaginations. Develop your story telling techniques, metaphors and images. Paint a picture of the future for people that leaves a clear image in their mind of a helpful future.

91. Look for evidence of the best in others. Catch them doing things right. Seek and you will find. Reinforce the behaviour through positive feedback so they will then be more likely to do it again.

92. Have a belief that everyone has a positive contribution to make. Don't allow hindering comments about other teams and functions to become the norm in your team.

93. Create a climate and environment where people are actively encouraged to get involved in new things, have a go and make mistakes in a safe way.

94. Ask people what they would like to experiment with bearing in mind that the world's greatest scientists often experimented many times before hitting on success. This will inspire people to give more of themselves. Plus it will lead to greater engagement as employees feel more confident that their ideas and contribution are valued.

✔ Time to Take Action

Which three tips will you take action on?
Use the table below to define your goals.

Tip no.	What specifically will you achieve?
By when?	Success measures
Tip no.	What specifically will you achieve?
By when?	Success measures
Tip no.	What specifically will you achieve?
By when?	Success measures
What else from this tips section do you want to remember?	

Involve Others

There can be a perception that as a senior person it could be a sign of weakness to ask for help. Involving others is actually a sign of being a Results Focused Thinker. It ensures more ideas, the use of appropriate abilities, quicker problem solving and good time management.

Plus, it gives the extra benefit of being a great employee engagement tool. What better way to engage others than to involve them. Additionally, it encourages people to work together and build strong relationships. An organisation that fosters positive relationships, good team working and a good atmosphere is likely to be more effective and profitable. This will show through low turnover of employees and low absenteeism. One of the key drivers of employee engagement is relationships at work.

"Do what you do so well that they will want to see it again and bring it to their friends."

Walt Disney

⭐ Tips for You

95. Start with the reasons. Whenever you start a new task or goal ask yourself the question, "What might be the possible reasons to involve someone in this activity?" This will ensure you then consider a diverse range of people to help you.

96. Identify who in your organisation could give you a fresh perspective and, at the same time, would really relish the opportunity to be asked to contribute ideas.

97. Involve your biggest critics and cynics. They might be the people who feel their ideas and opinions have not been valued in the past. Involving them will start to reverse that view and in return you will find an engaged employee with ideas they enjoy contributing.

98. Apply the broadest meaning of involving others to make it fun. Think creatively about who to involve, remembering that involving others doesn't necessarily mean they have to join you in the room. For example, how could you involve figures from history, well known personalities or fictional characters in your thinking? Consider the ideas and inspiration you could get by thinking about what they did and how they approached goals.

99. Take inspiration from unlikely places. Perhaps you are looking for more ideas about how to increase employee engagement and feel like you have exhausted the thinking in your organisation. Think creatively about who you could involve. For example:
   - Your neighbour - what does their organisation do to increase employee engagement?
   - Your partner - what happens in their organisation?
   - When you are supermarket shopping look closely for signs of employee engagement activity.
   - When you visit a supplier, ask what they do.

   The possibilities to learn are endless if you see everyone around you in a different way.

100. Seek feedback for yourself from a range of sources. Open up your blind spots. What might you learn about how you could change yourself to not only increase your own engagement but to increase the positive impact you have on others?

101. Choose the right champions to involve. Those that will help to make sure engagement captures hearts and minds. Get the buy-in of early adopters who are passionate about the idea of engagement and also about engaging and influencing others.

102. Benchmark the strength of your employee communication against that of customers, stakeholders and the community.

103. Become the go-to person for your work. If you're the expert, you will learn even more from the questions people ask of you.

104. Network with high performers. High performing people bring higher levels of engagement in their work. Get to the top of your game by talking with these people.

105. Become a 'trusted adviser'. Provide your views and share your business judgment to engage in higher level discussions.

106. Learn from those with adjacent skills to your skills. Adjacent skills are those that sit next to your skills. For example, if you know finance, learn from those that are experts in the bordering skill of financial reporting. Learning adjacent skills rounds out your knowledge and leads to engaged thinking.

107. Avoid taking responsibility for the attitude of others. However, identify if you can, what the issues might be. If you can understand why they are unhappy or frustrated, it can help you to compartmentalise and separate their moods from your work life. This will lessen the impact on you.

108. Reflect on your relationships at work. Assess the quality of these relationships and if they are at the level you desire.

109. Review your relationships with your team members. If any of the relationships are broken, then no amount of perks and

incentives will persuade employees to perform at top levels. Employee engagement is often a direct reflection of how employees feel about their relationship with the boss.

110. Seek to understand before being understood.

111. Make it okay to ask for help. Give yourself permission to do this. Asking for help will not only make others feel more involved but it could also save time and money.

✒ Tips for Leaders

112. Make it okay to ask for help. Yes, this is a repeat of the previous tip. However, this tip is about giving others permission to do this. Help to change any hindering thinking about involving others.

113. Identify your people with a great attitude. Typically 10% of people in the organisation will be go-getters and have helpful thoughts the majority of the time. 80% of staff are generally doing a good job and come to work to do that. And then there are the other 10% who do not care, they do not want to be there and generally have a high number of hindering thoughts about the organisation. Work with the go-getters to get them involved in making the differences that can help achieve your engagement goals.

114. Plan how the go-getters could possibly help you keep the 80% engaged and motivated.

115. Give your people a voice. Ask the people you lead to tell you what's right, what's wrong and what's missing from your thinking.

116. Keep an open mind. Truly consider others' ideas and opinions. Many leaders just want buy-in for their ideas. However, if you truly consider the ideas and opinions of the people you lead, you will connect with and engage them. Also, you will discover new information and insights that will help you make better decisions. Furthermore, the conversations will create a marketplace of possible ideas.

117. Use three pluses and a wish. When you need to share constructive criticism with someone you lead, remember the words of Mary Poppins "A spoonful of sugar makes the medicine go down". Add the sugar by communicating three positive comments that will encourage the person. Then the wish is whatever needs to change. Whenever possible, have this conversation in private.

118. Reach out in times of need. Over the course of life, we all experience difficult seasons, whether it's sickness, the death of a loved one, divorce or some other trying circumstance. Show you care. Send a card, a note, flowers, or say a few kind words. Above all acknowledge the difficulties faced. Remember that "a life not lived for others is a life not lived".

119. Introduce a system to facilitate two-way communication, including an option to provide anonymous feedback. Employees want to know that their opinions matter.

120. Show how the organisation is listening. Set up Senior Manager sessions to hear the voices and opinions of those at all levels of the organisation. Keep these relaxed and informal and avoid them becoming one way briefing sessions.

121. Target the highpoints. Ask employees questions about the highpoints in their careers so far and how to possibly make more highpoints happen to support the business.

122. Use technology to enable more people to be involved and get connected.

123. Investigate the use of mobile apps to create forums where people can discuss and debate ideas and share successes.

124. Embrace social media. You may not want people on Facebook at work, but a study of 18 to 24 year olds by Prescient Digital showed 39% would consider leaving if they were not allowed to access applications such as Facebook and YouTube. A further 21% said they would feel annoyed at such a policy. Consider how you can use social media to create a buzz and energy around your organisation's goals and communication messages.

125. Calculate the ratio between the amount of time you spend sat in your office or at your desk, versus the amount of time you spend outside of your office or away from your desk, talking, learning, inspiring others. As a general rule of thumb when it exceeds 2:1 in favour of the desk, it's time to take action to address the balance.

126. Involve people in the 'nice' jobs as well as the 'nasty' jobs. Do you always delegate the routine and less stretching jobs? Consider how you could share some of the excitement attached to other pieces of work. Remember 'excitement' and 'boring' are subjective words; what may be exciting for you could be very boring for someone else! Find out what ticks the excitement boxes for those you lead.

✔ Time to Take Action

Which three tips will you take action on?
Use the table below to define your goals.

Tip no.	What specifically will you achieve?
By when?	Success measures
Tip no.	What specifically will you achieve?
By when?	Success measures
Tip no.	What specifically will you achieve?
By when?	Success measures
What else from this tips section do you want to remember?	

Plan Priorities

We know from our Making A Difference research that people who achieve results do three things in relation to planning their priorities: They create a huge number of ideas through possibility thinking, prioritise those ideas according to what is important to be done to achieve the goal and then plan in time to achieve the priorities. We call this the 3P's: Possibilities, Priorities and Plan in time.

That probably sounds like common sense to you and it is! Imagine a team that:

- Struggles to generate ideas and new thinking.
- Often works on activities that are not priorities for the organisation.
- Has planning tools that generate fantastic looking action plans, but nobody plans in time to actually do the actions and so nothing moves forward at the pace required.

Contrast that with a team that can:

- Generate hundreds of possible innovative ideas to choose from in five minutes.
- Plans in the time to get the things done that are important for the achievement of the goal, and therefore achieves its results faster.

Which team do you think is more engaged?

These tips give you practical things you can do when prioritising and planning to help boost engagement.

"It is better to have enough ideas for some of them to be wrong, than to be always right by having no ideas at all."
Edward De Bono

✦ Tips for You

127. Train yourself to think in questions starting with 'what', 'how' or 'who'. This will keep you focused with a helpful and engaged mind-set. Plus in discussions with others the tone will also feel more results focused and proactive which is always good for engagement.

128. Hone your question design skills. You will be able to ask high quality possibility thinking questions that really engage people's imagination. This will give them permission to really let their imaginations run riot. The three most powerful starts to questions to ask begin like this:
    - What could we possibly…?
    - How could we possibly…?
    - Who could we possibly…?

129. Focus on quantity not quality. To have the greatest success and fun with possibility thinking you need to understand that the quantity of ideas is more important than the quality of ideas. This means that absolutely anything goes! Remember the quality will come when you prioritise.

130. Do your bit towards a 'Right First Time' ethic. Where someone in the chain of work cuts corners, delivers late, or gives ambiguous or unclear instructions it creates avoidable workloads for others. Ask yourself what needs to be done to get things right first time for every task.

131. Ask your manager what 'Right First Time' would look like.

132. Review the way you spend your time at work. Are you working on things that enable the maximum contribution from you? Are

you working on the things you enjoy that give you satisfaction? Keep a diary for a week about how you spent your time.

133. Align and simplify your priorities. Be sure you know what is important in achieving organisational objectives.

134. Take on a 5% challenge for yourself. Identify ways that you can recoup 5% of your working day. Start by calculating what 5% of your working day is in minutes. You'll probably find it's not a huge number but imagine what you could achieve and how you would feel if you had that time back for more rewarding activities.

135. Become known as someone who removes obstacles rather than adding them. Identify and remove any obstacles to employee engagement. Ask others what could possibly be removed or reduced to increase their level of engagement in the organisation.

136. Pick up the phone rather than email. Some organisations have non-email days. You don't have to wait for your organisation to do this. You can decide right now that you are only going to email when it's a necessity. See how many phone calls you can make today.

137. Prioritise your environment from time-to-time. Has it got untidy or do things need fixing? Do the posters on the wall need refreshing? How could you give the place a quick, low cost, yet impactful, facelift? If your environment looks tired and uncared for, might it be you feel the same way?

138. Speak up, get involved and offer ideas. Ask questions, as people always have a reason for what they do. If you don't understand, ask some questions and see if you can find out why that decision was made.

☆ *Tips for Leaders*

139. Use possibility thinking as a way to elicit great new ideas from your teams. This will help them feel involved. Plus it gives them a real opportunity to see how their ideas have shaped the direction of the organisation or have contributed to results in a tangible way.

140. Avoid asking questions starting with the word 'why' when discussing ideas that your team have come up with. People often hear that word and feel the need to justify or defend their idea. 'Why' is often heard as a judgmental or critical question, and therefore can be destructive to employee engagement.

141. Ask 'what if' to stimulate people's thinking. For example, "What if you were solely in charge of employee engagement, what action could you take right now to make a change?" The possibilities for 'what if' scenario questions are endless. See how many you and your team can come up with and watch the engagement in the topic increase!

142. Create a clear line of sight for people between what they work on and how that contributes directly to the achievement of the organisational goals. Consider how you can do this visually to really bring home that every contribution counts.

143. Create a culture where people can helpfully challenge work that does not align to a strategic objective or stated mission.

144. Ensure your team have clarity from you on what 'Right First Time' looks like to avoid them going through multiple re-iterations of the work.

145. Recognise and reward those that consistently apply a 'Right First Time' mind-set. We often hear about firefighting in organisations and the frustration this causes to people who quietly get on with doing a good job without the perceived glory attached to being a firefighter.

146. Review how your team spends its time. Ask them to keep a log of whether activities generated contribution and satisfaction. Identify together how you could change the nature or type of work to increase contribution and satisfaction.

147. Involve the team in a 5% challenge. How could they recoup 5% of their working day?

148. Make your meetings the engagement highpoint of the week. People spend a lot of time in meetings so they are a great opportunity to: celebrate, keep momentum going and give clarity. Make them exciting, surprising, dynamic, energetic and inspiring. You'll know that you've got there when you have full attendance and you don't have to chase people to attend.

149. Fix just one issue a day. Work on things that will improve your team's day-to-day work. This will build engagement and improvement. Find out what prevents them from doing a great job as it may be really easy for you to fix it for them. Then your team will look to identify issues more proactively. Help to foster an environment that gives them the ownership and accountability.

150. Make the time to go looking for conversation opportunities where you can make people smile, laugh and think differently.

151. Keep people future focused when prioritising and planning. Ask questions that are focused on the future you would like to see rather than recalled memories that are not helpful. The future belongs to people who see possibilities before they arrive!

152. Find new ways to get people fired up and excited about operational priorities by using different language. Use mission, challenge, quest or focus. You could introduce a seven-day challenge or a monthly mission.

153. Make it easier. People disengage if they are not given the resources, tools and support they need to do their best work. Talk and listen to your team, ask high quality questions to find out what could possibly help them do a better job. Then move mountains to get it for them. Making your team's life easier so they can achieve results faster should be one of your highest priorities.

154. Stop! Look at and listen to your environment. Do you hear a hubbub of excitement? Do you see people working in silos? Identify how you could randomly inject passion, enthusiasm and focus.

155. Prioritise and plan in time for formal one-to-one conversations. Have a look at how that time is divided between talking about tasks and talking about the person. Most leaders spend 100% of the time talking about tasks, which are of course important. However, imagine what difference it could make if you also spent time understanding how the person in front of you is feeling. Then identify ways to help them.

✔ *Time to Take Action*

Which three tips will you take action on?
Use the table below to define your goals.

Tip no.	What specifically will you achieve?
By when?	Success measures
Tip no.	What specifically will you achieve?
By when?	Success measures
Tip no.	What specifically will you achieve?
By when?	Success measures
What else from this tips section do you want to remember?	

Personal Responsibility

If we came into your organisation and asked your people who was responsible for employee engagement, what answer would we get? The HR department? The Senior Leadership Team? My Manager? The Employee Engagement Action Team? How many people would say that they were also responsible?

Where people have a greater self-awareness of the choices they can make in terms of their mind-set and thinking, and the impact those choices can have on those around them, you will get a personal responsibility culture. People will realise that they can do something about their own levels of engagement.

This series of tips is designed to help you, those that work for you and around you to take greater personal responsibility for employee engagement.

"If you think you are too small to make a difference,
try going to bed with a mosquito in your room."
Dame Anita Roddick

✶ Tips for You

156. "Be the change you want to see," said Mahatma Gandhi. Challenge yourself to find three new ways in which you can take personal responsibility today, tomorrow or the week after.

157. Ask yourself, "What and who am I waiting for?" Choose to wait no longer and consider what you could do to stop waiting and move this situation forward.

158. Remove the 'if only' phrase. Don't postpone your engagement efforts waiting for the 'if only'.

- If only the organisation would do this...
- If only my manager would recognise me...
- If only I had a different job...

Stop the 'if only' and do what you can with what you've got, wherever you are. Don't let what you cannot do interfere with what you can. A better question to ask yourself would be, "What could I possibly do about ..."

159. Profile the thinking of those who you believe already take personal responsibility in your organisation. Spend some time with them establishing their thinking. Take note of the questions they ask. Listen to how they talk about themselves, others or the situation. Notice, when they think about the past, what experiences they recall. Observe how they imagine the future.

160. Capture their thoughts and then use this as a benchmark for recruiting and developing others. Use this data to get a clear and practical description of what Personal Responsibility looks, sounds and feels like in the organisation.

161. To get a new results focused way of thinking, replace the word 'but' with 'and'.

162. Check your psychological contract with your organisation. Unlike the employment contract, the psychological contract is unwritten and based on your values and expectation about how you want to be treated. When the psychological contract is broken, it will feel as though trust has broken down. At this point people will withdraw their discretionary effort and levels of personal responsibility will reduce. Consider if you feel like your psychological contract with your organisation is broken.

163. Take personal responsibility to do something if your psychological contract feels broken. Discuss this with your manager and identify ways in which you can start to repair the relationship. Recognise you have choices and that it takes two to build a relationship.

164. Adopt a mind-set of Results Focused Thinking rather than 'problem solving'.

165. Focus on your contribution. Determine what part you will play. Understand that what you give is what you receive in return and that to be disengaged at work can often lead to disengagement elsewhere.

166. Be responsible whilst holding others accountable. Take responsibility for your own engagement whilst holding others accountable for their engagement.

167. Become the person who is known for doing something about the things that bother them.

Tips for Leaders

168. Listen, just listen! Give it a go now. With the next person who talks to you, put down your mobile phone, turn off your internal self-talk, look them in the eye and listen. Do you want people to engage? Then YOU rather than 'the company' will have to engage with them.

169. Carry out a self-analysis. As a leader consider your thinking, behaviours and actions. Identify any that lead people to feel unwilling or unable to take personal responsibility. Then take action to address that thinking or behaviours and change your actions.

170. Find out why people sometimes choose to take personal responsibility and sometimes they don't. And then seek to work with them to remove the barriers.

171. Showcase the situations where people have chosen to take, seek or create opportunities. In a victim culture people will choose to deny or ignore the opportunities around them to make a difference to themselves and the organisation. Take every opportunity to promote how people are making the most of opportunities in newsletters, on intranet sites, in briefings or wherever else is available.

172. Build personal responsibility into your values and competency frameworks.

173. Create an environment where people can take responsibility for developing themselves. Ensure this is acknowledged and rewarded.

174. Introduce the word 'choice' more, into your meetings, one-to-ones and communication. For example, "We're short of budget – what choices have we got?" Or, "Right now we haven't got enough people on board – what choices do we have?"

175. Ask someone what choices they are going to make today.

176. Give people the freedom to think and the freedom to act. Use a business issue that has been bugging them for years. Ask for their ideas and then empower them to implement. Show you are taking them seriously by giving them a Top Team sponsored 90-day challenge on the topic.

177. Have a personal responsibility player of the week award. Identify who has really practically taken personal responsibility this week. The award can be a simple token (such as a small

trophy) that gets passed from one person to another. Get the existing holder of the award to nominate the next to get some peer recognition going.

178. Notice how often you or others say, "I don't have enough time." People have choices about how they spend their time and sometimes managers steal that time. This could be through ineffective meetings, excessive bureaucracy, red tape or politics. Look back over your last week and ask; "How much time did you steal from your team?" Define yourself a goal about how you can give them that time back this week. It will probably be the greatest gift they receive this week (unless it's their birthday!).

179. Help people realise they have greater choices than they may at first imagine. Go through these steps:
   • Invite them to list all the items or factors that make up employee engagement for them
   • Ask them to sort these into items they can control, items they can influence and those that are a given, that is, the ones they have no control or influence over
   • Help them to define a goal around those things they can control
   • Work with them on those that they can influence
   • Encourage them to let go of those things that are a given
   • Always challenge the givens. Are they sure it is something they can't influence? Is there evidence that others can and do and therefore they could too?

180. Challenge assumptions. For example, people often cite a pay increase (or lack of) as a given. But if someone worked hard, exceeded their goals, was results focused in their thinking and a great team player – would they not be first in line for a pay increase?

181. Hold managers accountable. Focus on the required behaviours and ask managers to report results on actions they have taken to improve engagement in their teams.

182. Make employee engagement everyone's business and make it a regular part of doing business. Employee engagement needs to be owned by everyone in the organisation. To succeed it cannot be the responsibility of a single department, individual or team. Embed your employee engagement efforts into your regular ways of doing business.

183. Show your employees that you care for them. Take a minute to have a chat, ask them how their family are doing, how they are doing and how happy they are with their work. They will feel valued.

184. Get out there and support your employees! Do not sit in the office and wait for your results, you need to be out there where your people are, supporting them and helping them achieve their results. Make sure they know they get your support every day whenever needed.

185. Give thanks. Thank you for helping, for bringing a problem to your attention so you can get on top of it, for taking care of a client. When you thank people for something, there's a much better chance they'll do it again.

186. Make sure they know where you want to go. Meet with the people you lead as frequently as necessary to make certain they know where you want the group to go, how 'we' will get there, why it's important and what each individual's role is.

187. Create a mind-set of a genuine team. Encourage a culture where everyone who touches a piece of work, owns the whole

outcome, not just their piece of it. This will help people think in terms of the whole and not just the pieces.

188. Engage people in creating the desired future.

✔ *Time to Take Action*

Which three tips will you take action on?
Use the table below to define your goals.

Tip no.	What specifically will you achieve?
By when?	Success measures
Tip no.	What specifically will you achieve?
By when?	Success measures
Tip no.	What specifically will you achieve?
By when?	Success measures
What else from this tips section do you want to remember?	

Take Action & Measure Results

We have already mentioned earlier in the book the responsibility to increase employee engagement belongs to everyone. Also, without action, the probability that a difference will be made is, in a word, limited. These tips apply to you as an individual and as a leader.

> *"I dream, I test my dreams against my beliefs, I dare to take risks and I then execute my vision to make my dreams come true."*
> *Walt Disney*

189. Make inertia your enemy and momentum your friend! Wherever you see or feel it, challenge it with a helpful question such as, "What step could you take right now to get some momentum going?"

190. Consider banning phrases from your workplace that show a lack of taking action. Phrases such as, "We're waiting for…" could be replaced with, "In the meantime we took this action to keep things going."

191. Do something straight away to positively impact on your employee engagement score if you use a survey mechanism. Our experience shows the survey results come out and the next few months are spent analysing the results and doing more data collection. In the meantime, time has passed, the employees sense inertia, opportunities to get some traction on engagement is slipping way, and cynicism starts to take hold. So ask everyone to identify the one thing they will do to lift engagement in your organisation. Starting today. Yes, everyone…

192. Build employee engagement into your team meetings and one-to-ones in a simple and results focused way. For example it could be as simple as asking three questions:

- What did you do in the last week that raised your own levels of engagement?
- What have you done in the last week that has contributed positively to the engagement levels of others?
- What could I possibly do to help raise levels of engagement?

193. Challenge the mind-set that employee engagement is a task on a manager's 'to do' list. Invite them to see it is about changing the way that people think so they feel more able, equipped and willing to achieve the organisation's goals.

194. Keep a track of the number of ideas that get generated. A suggestion scheme with no suggestions is a sure sign of dis-engagement! People often stop making suggestions when they feel there is 'no point as no-one ever listens and takes our ideas on board'.

195. Actively look for suggestions that you can implement or develop. Value possibility thinking and reward the quantity of ideas as well as the quality. Someone who has taken the time to do some thinking was, at that point, engaged. Whilst they may not have come up with a business changing idea this time, next time they may do.

196. Use a metaphor to help you see the organisation's engagement levels in a different way. For example, imagine it was a person having a health check or a car having an MOT. Consider what different solutions and ideas you might uncover by thinking differently about the challenge.

197. Check you are measuring the right things. You could be tracking and measuring the implementation of a quantity of

employee engagement ideas but how do you know you are implementing the right things?

198. Turn the survey process on its head. Ask your team to come up with the questions! This will reveal the questions they want you to ask and give valuable insights into what's on their minds.

199. Define your actions in your improvement plan. Address your key issues and mind storm with your team ways of addressing these issues. Consider the possible ways you could communicate these improvement actions, and the possible reasons to involve other people.

200. Seek out the quick wins. That is, the quick and easy changes that can be made in the engagement journey. What are the key issues that have been identified that can be resolved or actioned easily and without too much effort? Ensure that your actions are visible so that you get buy-in from your employees as quickly as possible.

201. Track your progress, celebrate your success and learn from your challenges. 'What gets measured gets done' applies as much to employee engagement as to anything else in your organisation. As soon as you commit to improving engagement you will raise employee expectations for positive change. As change can be slow you need to make sure all of your progress is highlighted, celebrated, and built on as you move forward.

202. Remember to celebrate success. Take some time with the team to acknowledge when something has gone well and when things have been achieved.

The Case for Employee Engagement

Dorothy Perkins completed research which found that those environments characterised by high engagement (what they term 'high performing climates') demonstrated better financial performance.

Specifically, environments with high engagement demonstrated 12% higher growth in sales, delivered 10% improvements in operating savings, and experienced 35% lower stock loss. For a store with an average monthly turnover of £2.3 million the 12% higher growth could yield an annual financial gain of £445,000.

PART FOUR

LEADERSHIP THINKING FRAMEWORK

EMPLOYEE ENGAGEMENT
AT AN ORGANISATIONAL LEVEL

So far, we have focused on what employee engagement means for you as an individual and as a leader. Let's now consider this at an organisational level. More specifically how leaders within an organisation can take responsibility for creating the environment, conditions and culture that enable people to feel engaged.

Understand the drivers and recognise the current reality

Practitioner based research and literature such as that by CIPD and MacLeod & Clarke identifies the following drivers as key to employee engagement:

- Senior leadership communication and visibility
- Good quality line management
- Clear vision and line of sight
- Voice, the opportunity to share ideas and opinions and input into decision making
- Development opportunities
- Being ethical by treating individuals with respect, fairness and showing integrity
- The organisation demonstrating care and concern for employee well-being.

If these are cited as the conditions, or drivers promote the conditions in which engagement can thrive, then what does the current reality look like?

In most organisations today there are gaps among three groups of people:

- The Leaders – who can see what needs to be done but may not have their hands on the 'levers of change'

- The Workforce – who may have their hands on the 'levers of change', but simply cannot see the bigger picture for the organisation

- The Managers – who are typically caught in the middle.

Also you may hear conversations similar to this;

Leaders say things like – *"This is our vision and mission."*
The workforce reacts by saying – *"Sounds like blue sky to me, what does it mean?"*

Leaders say things like – *"You need to work smarter and harder."*
The workforce reacts by saying – *"We can't possibly work any harder."*

Leaders say things like – *"You are empowered."*
The workforce reacts by saying – *"More of that corporate management speak, here we go again!"*

Leaders say things like – *"We need to improve productivity."*
The workforce reacts by saying – *"We are the most productive we can be."*
Leaders react by saying – *"There will be no bonus payment this year."*

Managers sit in the middle trying to figure out which side they are on, whether they should be sending clearer messages to their 'workforce' or listening better so they can understand their leaders. They are torn between what the leaders want them to do and what the people that work for them need them to do.

Also, you may have customers not written into the conversation, wondering why nobody is focused on them, and what they have to do to get some service. Eventually they may go to another supplier where they will get the attention they expect.

This can often be the current reality in an organisation. The result of the feelings and actions of many people, the 35%-50% of employees who are disengaged at any one time, who are resentful to give the 'extra mile effort' and may feel a lack of support. Unfortunately many leaders do not face up to this current reality, yet it can be the starting point to create the right 'engagement' environment.

Introduce a different approach

The Go M.A.D.® Leadership Thinking Framework is a powerful tool for senior leadership teams who intend to implement changes in their organisations. It can be specifically used to understand the current reality, diagnose the issues, and then develop solutions to create the right environment, conditions and culture for engagement to thrive.

The Framework is an adaptation of the original Go M.A.D.® Framework and therefore relates directly to the principles and links already outlined.

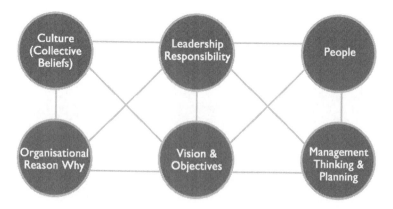

To help you and your leadership team with their thinking here are a set of questions that if answered, will increase your probability of success.

Leadership Responsibility

At the heart of the Framework is Leadership Responsibility, and if the right engagement conditions are going to be created, it is going to be the responsibility of the Leadership Team to put in place the processes and enablers to make it happen.

"Go to the people. Learn from them. Live with them. Start with what they know. Build with what they have. The best of leaders when the job is done, when the task is accomplished, the people will say we have done it ourselves."

Lao Tzu

? Ask Yourself

203. How could each and every member of the Leadership Team visibly demonstrate that they take their own engagement seriously?

204. How could the Leadership Team helpfully challenge each other and hold each other to account, when they see personal engagement is not being taken seriously? What formal and informal mechanisms could you put in place to do this?

205. How could each and every member of the Leadership Team visibly demonstrate that they have taken action on employee engagement in their own areas of responsibility each week, month and year?

206. How much 'air time' is given to the topic of employee engagement in leadership team meetings? Does it have equal weighting with other KPI's such as cost and quality? How could you elevate its status?

207. How would people, at all levels of the organisation, know that the whole Leadership Team takes responsibility for employee engagement?

208. How do the Leadership Team demonstrate that engagement is not just a buzz word, an initiative or flavour of the month?

209. How does the Leadership Team signal the importance of employee engagement through the implications and consequences for managers of, either great or poor employee engagement results?

210. To what extent is the competency of 'being engaged, and engaging' used as criteria by the Leadership Team for promotion, recruitment, succession planning and talent identification? How could you embed it in to these processes?

211. How much time does the Leadership Team spend informally with the workforce, away from their desk – discussing, listening and sharing?

212. How remote is the Leadership Team? How aloof are they perceived to be? What could you possibly do to remove any perceived physical barriers to a closer working relationship with all employees?

213. How could the Leadership Team show they can be trusted? A survey showed that only 47% of employees think their leaders are trustworthy (Towers Watson 2010 Global Workforce Survey). Trust is a combination of being credible, consistent

and having great relationships. Which of those factors do you and your leadership team need to focus on?

214. When initiating a change in the organisation, how could the Leadership Team possibly implement actions to avoid a dip in engagement as people experience transition? (Tip: the Go MAD Thinking publication, 'How to save time and money by managing organisational change effectively' has lots of ideas on how to do this.)

How much leadership responsibility is currently being demonstrated?

Which three questions are most important for you to think about?
Use the table below to capture your thoughts.

1	Q	
	A	
2	Q	
	A	
3	Q	
	A	
What else from this section do you want to remember?		

Vision & Objectives

This principle allows you to test whether the organisational vision and objectives are expressed with absolute clarity and consistency. Also, that the relevant people are able to describe and buy into them. It is not unusual for a set of individuals who make up a leadership team, to have contrasting views on the vision and its timescale. This difference of opinion can clearly have a knock on effect throughout the organisation.

"Where are we going lads?
To the toppermost of the poppermost."
John Lennon

? Ask Yourself

215. To what extent are the whole Leadership Team aligned on the vision and objectives for the organisation? How will you ensure it is cascaded with aligned messages?

216. How could the Leadership Team get other people involved at all levels of the organisation in the creation and development of the vision and its execution? What opportunities might this give for different perspectives?

217. How could the Leadership Team ensure they communicate the vision in a compelling way that captures hearts and minds?

218. How will the Leadership Team ensure the communication of the vision is a two-way process and demonstrate that feedback has been taken on board?

219. How will the Leadership Team acknowledge when goals are re-defined and changed? Recognise that your teams will see it as the goal posts moving so how could you provide clear and early explanations for this?

220. How could the Leadership Team utilise a range of communication processes to share open and transparent progress on objectives?

221. How could the Leadership Team pre-empt and address any hindering recalled memories by employees, about the vision and goals to avoid a 'here we go again' mind-set in the workforce?

222. How could the Leadership Team pre-empt and address any hindering imagined future thoughts by employees about the vision and goals – "This won't work, it'll be a disaster, that's never going to be achieved?"

223. How possibly could the Leadership Team do an inspiration check? To what extent have you inspired your people into action? What do they need from you to be more inspiring?

224. How could the Leadership Team use strategic business stories to add meaning to lifeless facts and figures?

225. How could the Leadership Team identify a strategy, initiative or objective that is not clearly understood by people in the business and communicate it more effectively?

226. What metaphor could possibly engage the people in the organisation in the emotion and drama of the business?

Time to Think as a Leader

Consider the story of your organisation

> *What is it?*
> *How effectively is the story communicated?*
> *What is the vision for the organisation?*
> *What do you understand your contribution to be?*

Which three questions are most important for you to think about? Use the table below to capture your thoughts.

1	Q	
	A	
2	Q	
	A	
3	Q	
	A	
What else from this section do you want to remember?		

Organisational Reason Why

This will stimulate your thinking around the internal and external drivers and motivators for improving the conditions for good engagement to thrive.

Internal drivers might include:
- Clear evidence of poor engagement
- Rising costs
- Poor productivity
- High absence rates
- Restructuring

External drivers might include:
- Different ways of working required
- Customer satisfaction
- Economic climate
- Competitor activity

"At IBM everybody sells! Every employee has been trained to think that the customer comes first – everybody from the CEO, to the people in finance, to the receptionists, to those who work in manufacturing. That is our vision."

Buck Rodgers, IBM

? Ask Yourself

228. What are the organisational reasons for improving the engagement of employees?

229. What is the current reality within the organisation?

230. How could the Leadership Team ensure that all employees understand the organisational Reason Why? Why does the organisation exist? What are its strategic aims? What role does it play in society and the world?

231. On a scale of 1 to 10 how passionate are the Leadership Team about increasing the levels of employee engagement in the organisation and taking the appropriate action?

232. What else will you have to understand about the reasons for improving the engagement of our employees?

233. How could the Leadership Team possibly let the people in the organisation know the Reason Why, in a language that makes sense to them and obtains their buy-in?

234. On a scale of 1 to 10 how important is it for the organisation to create the right conditions for employees to be engaged?

What are the implications of doing nothing?

Which three questions are most important for you to think about?
Use the table below to capture your thoughts.

1	Q	
	A	
2	Q	
	A	
3	Q	
	A	
What else from this section do you want to remember?		

Culture (Collective Beliefs)

Every individual holds a set of beliefs about themselves and their workplace. Those beliefs may be unchallenged assumptions and not necessarily facts. Plus they may be engrained having been formed over many years. Regardless of the origin and validity of these beliefs, people will act in accordance with them. An organisational culture is the collective sum of your employees' beliefs (which can of course be helpful or hindering) and the resulting behaviours.

An employee engagement culture could therefore be defined as one where there is evidence of;

- **THINKING** hard about the job and how to do it better
- **FEELING** positive about doing a good job
- **ACTING** to take opportunities to discuss work-related improvements with others at work.

"Whistle while you work."

The Seven Dwarves – Snow White

? Ask Yourself

235. How could the Leadership Team possibly champion, reward and role model the culture required for good employee engagement to exist?

236. How could the Leadership Team role model behaviours that support the direction of the organisation?

237. What hindering thoughts do the Leadership Team have that will impact on their confidence to implement the changes required?

238. What would be a more helpful thinking approach?

239. How would people at all levels of the organisation answer the question, "How does what I do fit into where the company is heading?"

240. How well are senior leaders and managers developing their skills so that they can translate strategy to teams and individuals?

241. When initiating change, how could the feelings of uncertainty, unfairness or powerlessness in the workforce be managed to avoid a dip in engagement? What role could the Leadership Team play?

242. How can the Leadership Team ensure that ALL staff believe that their work is meaningful? Giving meaning to someone's work is about telling and showing them how their tasks contribute to the aims and story of the business. To do this you need a simple, tangible business mission and story. The perfect example is the NASA janitor who told the President of the United States, John F. Kennedy, his job was to "Help put a man on the moon."

243. How can leaders ensure that employees have a real sense of creating value? Engaged people want to make a difference and people who want to make a difference are engaged.

244. To what extent are the leaders taking the opportunity to connect the organisation's vision to the job of every single employee? Everyone should be able to see the importance of their part in the bigger picture of the organisation. The result will be accountable and engaged people.

245. What are the possible tasks that you could take to develop an open and transparent culture?

246. What possible assumptions might the workforce be holding related to the way that you communicate?

At your next team meeting, ask your colleagues about the highlights of their careers so far. Ask them for their opinion on how to make more highpoints happen.

Which three questions are most important for you to think about? Use the table below to capture your thoughts.

1	Q	
	A	
2	Q	
	A	
3	Q	
	A	
What else from this section do you want to remember?		

Management Thinking & Planning

This explores what management activity needs to take place to achieve effective employee engagement. This would include determining to what extent the thinking and activities of the Management Group promote the environment to foster an engaged workforce.

"Words can be short and easy to speak.
Get them right and their echo can be endless."

Mother Theresa

? Ask Yourself

247. Think inside the box, what could managers do differently, within the boundaries that they have been given, to engage their employees?

248. What are the possible ways that managers could effectively use relevance to engage? For example, using different techniques to translate the vision.

249. How could you encourage managers to consider as many options as possible to open their minds to new ways of doing things?

250. What could the Leadership Team do differently to release or create time for managers to enable them to concentrate on new actions and behaviours?

251. What could you stop doing to create capacity so that employees can concentrate on new actions and behaviours?

252. What possible ways could managers encourage individual thinking and creativity?

253. In what ways could managers challenge the status quo to support the development of an engagement culture?

254. What possible obstacles might managers and leaders face in the organisation when developing a clear line of sight between organisational vision and individual employee goals? How might these be overcome?

255. In what ways could the Leadership Team support managers in 'checking the temperature' of the organisation?

256. How could you identify what is so obvious that it is invisible, and then take action to change it?

257. In what ways could a relationship between employee engagement and innovation within the organisation be developed?

258. If you were asked by an employee, "When you hear the term employee engagement, what do you think and feel, and what images come to mind?" How would you respond?

Time to Think as a Leader

What engagement activity is taking place in the organisation?

Is the quality of management thinking and planning helping to create the right environment for engagement to happen?

What possible tasks could be carried out to help foster the right environment?

Which three questions are most important for you to think about? Use the table below to capture your thoughts.

1	Q	
	A	
2	Q	
	A	
3	Q	
	A	

What else from this section do you want to remember?

 **People**

Paying attention to this principle will widen your leadership team's thinking about the range of people who need to be engaged and bought into the organisational goals, plus, the different strategies that might be required to involve them. This could include how you might segment employees into different groups, who might require different types and frequency of communication. For example, in your organisation there might be different leadership groups, different functional groups, and representative bodies.

Most people want to feel good about themselves, what they do, whom they work for, and what their organisation stands for.

As well as employees, you could consider customers, consumer groups, shareholders, suppliers and other strategic partners or alliances.

"The Customer Comes Second: Put Your People First and Watch 'em Kick Butt."

Hal Rosenbluth, Rosenbluth International

? *Ask Yourself*

259. Who are the different people (either individuals or groups) that need to be 'engaged'?

260. How could you and the Leadership Team possibly create a clear line of sight from your vision to the individual goals of these people?

261. In what ways could you possibly make the physical working environment stimulating, so that people feel inspired to work with, and for you?

262. How could the Leadership Team identify incentives which could be put in place to encourage others or yourself to become engaged in the workplace?

263. How could you encourage people to work in a co-operative manner, encouraging shared responsibilities, and collective accountabilities?

264. When was the last time you asked an employee what engages them?

265. What are you doing each day to model enthusiastic employee engagement for your people?

266. What could the Leadership Team possibly do to identify which parts of the organisation believe they are being treated unfairly?

267. What have you done today to support or connect with a colleague and how could you possibly improve this?

268. How overwhelmed do you think your people are? How much is this feeling affecting their level of engagement? What could you do to change it?

What one action if taken would have the biggest impact on the engagement of people within the organisation?

Which three questions are most important for you to think about?
Use the table below to capture your thoughts.

1	Q	
	A	
2	Q	
	A	
3	Q	
	A	
What else from this section do you want to remember?		

Take Action and Measure Results

Using the Leadership Thinking Framework to develop a culture of engagement is not a one-off event. Make it part of your ongoing review processes, using it as a diagnostic tool to determine which principle needs the greatest attention. Then act on it.

"Take time to deliberate; but when the time for action arrives, stop thinking and go in."

Napoleon Bonaparte

 Time to Think as a Leader

What opportunities do you have in your business where applying the Go M.A.D.® Leadership Thinking Framework would help improve the levels of engagement from your employees?

Using the Framework as a diagnostic tool, which principles do you think need the greatest attention right now to help you with your engagement challenges?

What actions will you take to strengthen or reinforce those principles that you have identified as needing attention?

The Case for Employee Engagement

Work by **Serco and Aon Hewitt** looking at 274 Serco client contracts demonstrated a longitudinal relationship between employee engagement and the Net Promoter Score (NPS), a measure of customer loyalty. Those contracts serviced by employees whose engagement had improved over the year had NPS scores 24% higher than those employees whose engagement had declined.

SUMMARY

We said in the foreword to the book, 'Do we really need another book on employee engagement?' Hopefully we have shown you why. We wanted to show you the '**How to**' about employee engagement rather than the '**What is**' employee engagement.

Also to give you the opportunity to consider this for yourself, as a leader and from the organisational perspective.

We'll leave you with the two questions posed at the start of the book.

As an individual employee, ask yourself this question:

'What could I be doing to take personal responsibility for my OWN engagement?'

As a **leader** (a colleague or peer) ask yourself this question:

'What could I be doing to influence the engagement of OTHERS?'

Note: You may also wish to read the complementary Go MAD Thinking publication, 'How to save time and money by managing organisational change effectively' to understand the secret to managing change whilst maintaining levels of engagement.

NOTES

ABOUT THE AUTHORS

Jo Hutchinson started her career in retail before moving into HR Management with a variety of blue chip organisations across a number of industry sectors.

Now a Senior Go MAD Thinking Engineer, Jo brings her experience and expertise to a variety of leadership, change and business improvement programmes with a range of clients across the world. She is also the co-author of 'How to save time & money by managing organisational change effectively' and 'How to make a difference by transforming managers into leaders.'

An experienced senior leader, coach and facilitator, Jo has been able to help many individuals make a difference through her passionate advocacy of the Go M.A.D.® Results Focused Thinking Approach.

Rob Huntington has had extensive experience over the last 20 years in senior positions within the Public Sector. He led multi-disciplinary teams on high profile reviews of service delivery within local authorities, emergency and health organisations. His passion for innovation, the creative use of resources and the generation of possibilities to improve the quality of services in all sectors remain his key drivers.

Working worldwide with Go MAD Thinking, he drives programmes to develop cultural transformation, manage organisational change and develop leadership thinking. Rob is passionate about developing people to make a difference through access to pragmatic and straightforward tools and techniques.

ACKNOWLEDGEMENTS

Special thanks go to the group of Senior Leaders who joined us for an Organisational Development Thinking Day on the topic of employee engagement. Their discussion, thoughts and debate helpfully provoked our thinking on this topic, much of which is included in the book. In addition, members of the Employee Engagement LinkedIn group contributed some great ideas to help develop the Top Tips.

We would like to thank the following for making a difference with their contributions:

> Alasdair Moore – Rolls-Royce plc
> Amanda Lammonby - ATS
> David Morris – Rolls-Royce plc
> Diane Papworth – Kraft Europe
> Emma Caudwell – EDF Energy
> Jane Linnell – ATS
> Laurence Ibrahim – GE Capital UK
> Mark Szulc – Ocean Spray
> Matt Burton – Alliance Boots
> Mick Roberts – Alliance Boots
> Sue Petrie – University of Derby
> Suzanne Beattie - OSyS
> Viliana Dzhartova – Rolls-Royce plc

Also, a special thanks to those who took the time to provide feedback on the proof copy of this book. Their comments and ideas were greatly appreciated and have helped to shape this edition.

HAS THIS BOOK LEFT YOU WANTING TO KNOW MORE?

If you are seeking to make a difference within your organisation and would like to have a discussion about any aspect of applying Go M.A.D.® as a results focused approach to employee engagement, leadership thinking, organisational change, business improvement, management development or cultural transformation, then please contact us and a Go MAD Thinking Engineer will be happy to discuss possibilities.

Log on to www.gomadthinking.com to find out more about Jo, Rob, the Go MAD Thinking Team and how they have been helping organisations to make a difference for over 15 years.

Also at www.gomadthinking.com you can sign up to our newsletter for tips and to gain access to other useful resources.

Complete the exercises within the book to develop your individual thinking

Download and listen to our free top ranked podcast series 'Thinking for Business Success' on iTunes. These are short, practical and entertaining, covering many topics, including a series of podcasts relating specifically to employee engagement.

Contact Us

Go MAD Thinking
Pocket Gate Farm
Off Breakback Road
Woodhouse Eaves
Leicestershire
LE12 8RS
United Kingdom

T: +44 (0)1509 891313
F: +44 (0)1509 891582
E: info@gomadthinking.com
W: www.gomadthinking.com
Twitter: @gomadthinking

Discover more ways to make a difference
Other Go MAD Thinking publications include:

Go MAD – the art of making a difference
The original Go M.A.D.® personal effectiveness book and a great introduction to the Go M.A.D.® Results Focused Thinking System

Go MAD About Coaching
Over 200 powerful coaching questions, plus tips, tools, techniques and templates. The managers' guide for helping others to make a difference. Includes audio CD (via voucher)

How to save time and money by managing organisational change effectively
Essential tools to unlock the secrets of change and effective transition

How to make a difference by transforming managers into leaders
255 thought provoking tips to create passionate leaders who make a difference and love what they do

Who's driving your bus?
An inspirational story about the power of the Go M.A.D.® Thinking System

How to avoid the training trap
101 ways to ensure that development gives a great return on investment and really makes a difference

Go MAD About Negotiating
Achieving results through influencing the thinking of others

How to create a culture of commitment in your contact centre
101 tips that will make your call centre a great place to work

E-books:

- available to download from www.gomadthinking.com

How to achieve what you want, when you want!
Seven powerful principles of successful thinking for work, life and everything

How to develop a personal passion
Practical tips and insights to increase your motivation to achieve

How to determine what you want and when you want it
Pragmatic steps to leaping into the top 5% of goal definers

How to produce plentiful possibilities, pressing priorities and perfect plans
Quick and easy tips to plan success, eliminate time wasting and get started

How to create a self-belief that you can and will achieve
Powerful insights into building the confidence to succeed

How to get others on our side
Definitive guidelines on involving others and getting them on your side to achieve what you want

How to make personal choices and take responsibility
Insightful ideas to help you own your thoughts and actions and increase probability of success

How to guarantee your success
Clear and simple advice on challenging your thinking and tips on taking actions and measuring results

Making a difference workbook
30 activities and exercises for successful thinking about work, life and everything

Made in the USA
Charleston, SC
12 October 2014